Do Not Marry for Love

Do Not Marry for Love

THE COLLECTED POEMS

Wayland Bryant Jackson

Charleston, SC
www.PalmettoPublishing.com

DO NOT MARRY FOR LOVE

Cover Art:
Watercolor painting by Wayland Bryant Jackson of his wife of 62 years,
Betty Jane Hollandsworth Owens Jackson

Second Edition

Library of Congress Control Number: 2023905509

Paperback ISBN: 979-8-8229-1491-9
eBook ISBN: 979-8-8229-2377-5

A not boring Preface with a bizarre Offer

Emerging on the literary scene at 92, the poet includes subjects ranging from birth, love, marriage, and death to pigs, frogs, chickens, and polliwogs. Believing that poems, like notes on paper, must be heard to be appreciated, he makes an unusual offer. If you buy the book, read it aloud, and find nothing that inspires, instructs, or amuses you, mail your copy to the address below for a full refund. Do not feel guilty that you are cutting into his old-age retirement account. That's okay. On the other hand, if you like it, help a starving poet, and recommend it to a friend.

Sincerely,

Wayland Bryant Jackson
2203 West Norwich Avenue
Fresno CA 93705-1230
(559) 346-9908

Table of Contents

Introduction: On Poetry

When they see poetry coming, some people lock their hearts, their minds, and their wallets. They are confident they will not understand it, but if they do, they are just as sure it will bore them to tears, real tears. Their reactions are due to a gross misunderstanding.

Poetry, like music, should strike the ear, not the eye. Words on paper are no more poetry than notes on paper are music. Reading a poem without hearing the words is like taking sheet music to your bedroom and leaving your guitar on the couch. Music comes alive only when it's heard, like Elton John playing the Million Dollar Piano at Las Vegas, or the New York Philharmonic fiddling as if their lives depended on it.

Read aloud and thrill to the music of Elizabeth Barrett Browning's serenade to her husband:

How do I love thee? Let me count the ways.
I love thee to the depth and breadth and height
My soul can reach, when feeling out of sight
For the ends of being and ideal grace . . .

Listen to the hoofbeats of Alfred, Lord Tennyson's "Charge of the Light Brigade," about 600 British cavalry riding into a trap to be slaughtered:

. . . Into the valley of Death
Rode the six hundred . . .
. . . Theirs not to make reply,
Theirs not to reason why,
Theirs but to do and die.

Listen to a nation writhing in pain as you read aloud, "O Captain, My Captain," Walt Whitman's lament at the death of Lincoln at the close of the American Civil War:

. . . The ship has weather'd every rack,
the prize we sought is won,
The port is near, the bells I hear,
the people all exulting,
While follow eyes the steady keel,
the vessel grim and daring;
But O heart! heart! heart!
O the bleeding drops of red,
Where on the deck my Captain lies,
Fallen cold and dead.

All poetry is not for all people, just as all music is not for everybody. Play an aria from a Verdi opera and a foot-stomping ballad about a runaway hound dog in succession. You're unlikely to enjoy both equally. My choice would be to leave the dog alone. If he loves you, he will return.

The Paris premier of a Wagner opera resulted in riots in the streets. Parisiennes did not care for it. If the ear rejects the music, move on just as you would put down one book and reach for another.

I contend that the purpose and function of the poet is to probe our minds and emotions, then to help us put into words what we think and feel. Of course, not everyone will get the same picture, but everyone gets something listening to the words of Robert Frost in "Stopping by Woods on a Snowy Evening:"

. . . The woods are lovely, dark, and deep,
But I have promises to keep,
And miles to go before I sleep . . .

It's about the music of the words. I look at a rainbow and say, "Beautiful." William Wordsworth looked at a rainbow and wrote:

My heart leaps up when I behold
A rainbow in the sky:
So was it when my life began;
So is it now I am a man;
So be it when I shall grow old,
Or let me die! . . .

So, a poem is words—one after another—that, when read aloud, make us feel, in the midst of darkness, like someone lit a match. It's like a movie that is so good we forget we're watching a film, or a book so engrossing we inhabit another time and place for a season. The sound of a great poem carries us along like the crest of a 20-foot wave on Honolulu's north shore! Awesome, dude, hang ten!

Do Not Marry for Love

Placing a Wedding Ring, photo by Petar Milošević

Do not marry for love.
Like the tide, love flows and ebbs.
Like a selfish toddler, it's never satisfied.
Like a fire, fuel spent, it dies out.

Do not marry for love.
Like a fever, love will overcome you,
Like the awe of Christmas time
When only the wrappings remain.

Do not marry for love.
You are not “prince and princess.”
No one lives “happily ever after.”
Love does not conquer all.

Marry her for the light in her eyes,
The reflection of the sun through her hair,
Her intoxicating smell, her beguiling smile.
Marry her for the shape of her hands.

Marry her for the tip of her nose,
Marry her for the warmth in her voice,
Marry her because you match,
Because she is strong.

Then comes love
That knows neither tide nor season,
That will not go away, that needs no stoking,
And blankets the soul like a snowy benediction.

Polliwog

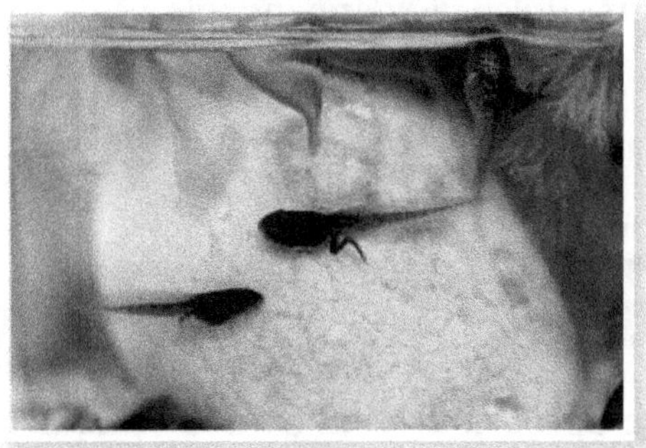

Tadpole

My life began in a small, watery world,
Mostly head, with a wriggling tail.
I swam, but not by choice.
I couldn’t help it. It’s my nature.
Any bully or predator
Could take me out in a single gulp.

The winds of change swept in
Like a sudden storm.
Someone was reorganizing me!

I had new cravings, a new appetite.
My tail! My tail
Was shrinking away!
What are these new appendages?
Where did I get these lungs, and for what?
For screaming? For singing?
Look at my legs!

Now, I move with equal ease on land and water.
I laugh uproariously at my baby pictures.
Did I ever look like *that?*
My mirror says, "What a handsome dude."
Muscles Zeus would be proud of,
A smile as wide as the Grand Canyon.
Soulful eyes that say,
"Don't you just love me?"

Tree frog

There is no darkness so dark . . .

There is no darkness so dark
As the darkness of a mind that is closed.
No window permits a sliver of light.
No new air steals through cracks or crevices
Stuffed with dogma and creed.
Smoking wicks cast misshapen shadows on barren walls.

There is no light so bright,
So frightening, so promising
As when unshuttered portals admit snow-blinding light,
A fearful vista of doubts and questions
Swirling pell-mell among endless truths
In quest of a terminus cloistered beyond imagination.
Better to battle the dragons of doubt
Than lie benumbed in a blanket of security.

The Sea of Uncertainty

OZ Goose Sailing Dinghy

On the ISLE OF CERTITUDE
Citizens with Answers display an omnipresent scarlet “A”

On class rings, tie-dyed T-shirts, and baseball caps,
On amulets, billboards, and street signs.

ORTHODOXY does away with budding queries,
Corrects language, and enforces laws
In libraries overflowing with scriptures,
Creeds, and how-to books,
Giving guided tours of chiseled tombstones:
THOUGHT, CONJECTURE, DISCUSSION,
And the most fearsome, QUESTIONS.

HERESY laps at the shores
Where bikini-clad DOCTRINES
Lounge on CANONICAL blankets
Beneath ECCLESIASTICAL umbrellas,
Sending siren calls across the waves:
“Come back . . . Be safe . . . Be saved.”

From a parapet atop the city wall,
North, south, east, and west,
DOGMA scans the SEA OF UNCERTAINTY,
Tracking vessels named FEARLESS and INTREPID
Riding 100-foot crests of HOPE,
Disappearing in troughs of DESPAIR.

The sea teems with questions:
Whale questions, minnow questions,
Shark questions, goldfish questions
That animate the lone ADVENTURER
Navigating tides of TOLERANCE
Over reefs of TRADITION,
Unwrapping gifts from mixed bags
Of the UNKNOWN and the UNKNOWABLE,
Tasting delights and mysteries
As winds waft welcome waves of DOUBT
Across the SEA OF UNCERTAINTY.

Two Men and a Fish

A certain man rose up early,
took his son to holy worship
where anthems filled a vaulted dome.
White robed clerics pointed skyward,
unraveling God and mysteries,
while in the attic of his restless mind,
in a dusty, cobwebbed corner,
his love of fishing stirred.

Another man rose up early
and took his son to the lake.
They rowed, dropped anchor, baited hooks,
and waited in silence.
Colors, like diamonds, rubies, and amethysts,
danced on shimm'ring waters—
a stained-glass window come alive,
like Resurrection Day.

*Fall foliage colors lake reflections,
West Virginia, photo by ForestWander*

The Birth of an Idea

Like a fetus in utero,
IDEA runs a maze
From synapse to synapse,
In search of light and days,

An amorphous figure
In a darkened room
Longing for release
From its tiny mind-womb

Full-term or preemie,
It comes to make its case
In the marketplace of ideas
Among the human race,

Steps into the footlights
To try out for a role,
To bare before an audience
Its mentor's soul.

Recites its part before
A faceless, restive crowd,
No hidden prompter
Needed—or allowed.

Speaks in words,
Sentences, and punctuation,
Demonstrates its form
And use in conversation.

Scene one, a duel joined.
STATUS stalks its prey.
Change and fear of change,
Haunt it night and day.

Suffering mortal wounds,
STATUS pleads its case while dying.
IDEA wins the day
With hardly any trying.

Now public property,
IDEA descends like rain,
No path, no charted course,
No heavenly domain.

Pauses not to lick its wounds,
To lie down or to sleep.
The world its field
To till, to sow and reap,

Moves freely
With no need for fixed foundation,
Stakes its claim
In humankind's store of information.

IDEA flexes its muscles and,
Short or long of breath,
A star is born and stands alone—
Or dies a natural death.

The Poet and the Musician

God will not sit for a painting,
Nor spring from a sculptor's hand,
But the Poet makes God a King, a shepherd,
A Lamb, a lion, light, darkness, garden and gardener.
Says the poet, "Kiss the hand that writes the words.
Without them, God would not exist."

Through open windows pours an angry uproar.
Voices chant, "Poets be damned!"
Signs with quarter notes and treble clefs pulse.
"Music is the door to the sublime."
The Musician declares, "When my notes fill the air,
The gates of heaven swing wide."

The poet chides himself, "I hear
Valkyries galloping off to Valhalla,
Carrying tens of thousands on the backs of music."
The musician concedes, "How soft the words,
'The Lord is my shepherd.'"
Both turn spirit into sound, and sound into spirit.

Fresno: The Musical

Musicians take their places,
The oboe tunes the orchestra,
Lights dim, and Mother Nature
Strides to the podium, raises her baton,
And sweet melody washes over the valley.

The arc she traces calls up springtime.
Trees proud and tall,
Shrubs and bushes fully robed,
Fresno flaunts her emerald,
Her mint, jade, and lime.

Celebrating the hours,
Violins, violas, and cellos
Serenade shrubs, leaves, and blossoms,
The lushness of Mother Earth.
Her bosom bursts with color.

In the hands of a master composer,
Foliage reaches a crescendo.
Strings catch fire, colors shift
As, eyes lowered, Fresno blushes
To purple, yellow, and red.

Mother Earth blows colder,
And Fresno sways seductively,
Drops a leaf or two.
Then, more and more float
Down into open arms,

Leaving bare limbs outstretched
For all the world to see,
Naked and unashamed.
The sky darkens.
The song turns ominous.

Winter melds into a Russian folk tune,
Dark and doleful,
While Fresno shivers and trembles
With the heart of a jilted lover
Listening for spring.

On an Early, Cloudless Morning

Skein of pink-footed geese in 'V', by Apricaria

Driving south on 41,
Passing Bullard, nearing Shaw,
In my windshield's orange glare,
High in heaven's canvas blue,
Moved a mystic, V-shaped line,

Stroking sky, a dream-like wave,
Pushing waking air aside,
Necks outstretched, in perfect flight.

As the undulating boomerang
Disappeared in morning's haze,
My heart leaped and sang with joy,
And I longed to be with them.

If I Return

Passer domesticus flying, by SimonWaldherr

After I die,
After my body is lowered into the grave,
Burnt into ashes,
Or fed to wild dogs,

If I return,
May it be as a bird.

Lifespan of months or years, no more,
Driven by season, snow, and storm,
Gleaning with never a Sabbath rest,
Falling to earth with none to mourn,
Banished from thought by all but God,

They sail on placid lakes of blue,
Fly with full-feathered wings,
Swim in heaven's crystal vault,
Split clear skies without a sound,
Surf invisible winds and clouds.

Bound by nature's laws alone,
They soar . . .
And soar . . .
And soar . . .

After I die,
If I return,
May it be as a bird.

When I Was 19

When I was 19,
Twenty looked like an endless party,
Fun, with few responsibilities.
I could vote, be legal in a bar,
Afford a snazzy car.

When I was 29,
Thirty looked like a doomsday book:
Marriage, kids, the daily grind,
Mortgages and in-laws.
Given a choice, I would have waited.

When I was 49,
Fifty brought a plethora of changes,
Not the least of which was becoming a beggar.
"Do you give a senior discount?"
A good start on a middle-aged paunch.

When I reached 79,
Nearing the edge,
Past my "use by" date, I got lucky.
Eighty rolled over me like a gentle ocean wave.

Now I'm 89,
I'll bag my limit,
Catch as many fish as the law allows,
And shoot my final arrow.
I'll not be surprised by Death,
And only slightly inconvenienced.

David Was Only 19

The Drive Up

Like a speeded-up movie,
Swaying to a tune played on his nerves
By rushing, wild winds,
Dazzled by his own daring,
Eyes a-twinkle,

Ford Bronco Raptor

David darted up to Aubury,
Tearing through mountain turns,
Sailing past granite boulders,
Douglas firs, and manzanitas,
Red Ford Bronco and black asphalt
Sweeping by each other in a blur.

The Return

Like a silent ghost,
A pale blue ambulance,
In stately reverence,
Measured quiet miles,
Descending without a sound,
Making full stops at each crossing,
Like a blind man with a white cane.

An Old Man & a Young Man

An old man rises from sweet sleep,
Eggs over easy, buttered toast, marmalade,
Orange juice and coffee black,
Dons a ribbon-laden, double-breasted jacket,
Gives the little wife a peck on the cheek,
Walks briskly to a chauffeured car,
Sits back, briefcase at his side,
Commutes a well-trodden path
Past gray monuments guarded by wind-whipped flags,
To an oddly-shaped building with a war room.

Colludes with other old men around a monitor,
Moves men, ships, and munitions
Like a croupier moves chips on a craps table,
Orders black ops ten thousand miles away
In deserts, mountains, jungles, and cities.

Retired Col. Dick Camp, author of "The Devil Dogs at Belleau Wood," speaks with Sgts. Ricardo Quintanilla, Brandon McCormick and Jarred Bluecoat about Marines who fought in the World War I battle at Belleau Wood, photo by Sgt. Lisa R. Strickland

A light lunch, counting calories,
Washing hands in the executive washroom,
Drying on a soft white linen towel.
Tips smiling Sam, who brushes his shoulders,
Tidies up his desk, shuts down the computer.

The sun trails yellow, orange, maroon.
The same straight-backed monuments
On the opposite side this trip.
Strolls in to spouse and fillet mignon,
Feeds dogs and Fantail goldfish,
Catches up on the news and wanders to the bedroom.
Sleeps the sleep of innocents.

On the opposite side of the circle,
A well-trained unit boards transport,
Charges mach speed to a nameless target.
A grim lieutenant, baby-face blackened,
Code name, Panda—his wife's idea—
Flips through a mental album
Of her and Annie,
Who started kindergarten today.
A blood memory nauseates him,
But he holds it down.
Night vision goggles ready,
Knife hilt above its scabbard.
Re-checking the full magazine,
Fingers the trigger on his weapon.
Hovering three feet above earth,
In a sandstorm raised by rotor blades,
Go! Go! Go!

Charging through the open courtyard,
A horizontal hailstorm of lead,
Bullets ripping human flesh,
Acrid stench of gunpowder.

Grabbing papers, computers, notebooks.
Pockmarked walls, a woman covering herself,
A wide-eyed, blood-splattered child
Holding a doll by its arm at her side.
A slaughterhouse filling up with fresh meat.

A door hurtles open.
A sudden burst of automatic fire,
Bullets spraying the room.
Shooter's finger locked on firing mechanism,
The weapon dancing like a marionette.
Enemy shredded.
Panda down!

Men panting like bears in heat
Hurry Panda to the Chinook.
Blood like a mountain spring
Gushes from his wound.
Sargent: ***Getusouttahere!***

A Czech soldier with the 1st Company, 41st Mechanized Infantry Battalion carries a U.S. Soldier with the 173rd Airborne Brigade Combat Team Sept. 2, 2014, during Saber Junction 2014 at the Joint Multinational Readiness Center in Hohenfels, Germany. Saber Junction is a U.S. Army Europe-led exercise designed to prepare U.S., NATO and international partner forces for unified land operations, photo by SKC Tyler Kingsbury

To Hell With You

Dedicated to my friend, Bob Jones.
After Bob died, an autopsy determined
he did not have a single prejudiced bone
in his entire body.

I'm Caucasian, white, to you.
And if you're not, to hell with you.

I'm an American, born in the U. S. of A.
If you're not, to hell with you.

I speak English, the Southern version.
You no *comprende*? To hell with you!

I'm male. I know who's boss,
And it's not you, so, to hell with you.

I've got degrees in spades rolling off my mortarboard.
Never had a mortarboard? To hell with you!

I'm literate. Yes, literate.
Don't know what that means? To hell with you!

You wear a towel; you veil your face?
Not in this country! To hell with you.

I'm straight, like God intended!
I hear you're not. To hell with you!

I'm a believer in the only true right way.
You're not? To hell with you!

God bless me; God bless mine.
If you're different—To hell with you.

Red devil

Should Auld Acquaintance

Times Square New Year's celebration, Dec. 31, 2011,
New York, NY, US, by Nichole A. Hall

The New Year's ball descends,
While a million bits
Of white and colored confetti,
Tossed from roofs of skyscrapers,
Tumble helter-skelter, pell-mell,
Prancing madly in mid-air
Like dancing comic clowns,
A riot of aerial acrobats
Performing Olympian stunts.

Above the maze—
Black silence.

The Day I Walked Out

Photo by Bob Smith

Gone, the roof over my head, a car in the driveway,
Parents, spouse, children, grandchildren.
No more evenings watching TV in the den,
No vacation, pension, or trips to Disneyland.

No more house payments,
Car payments, insurance premiums.
No state or federal taxes,
Never punch in, never punch out.
No audits. No online bill paying.
No will. No funeral arrangements.

Collect aluminum cans and plastic bottles,
Spend my go-power on my shopping cart,
Watch out for the deranged, druggies, and pervs.
Be my own nurse and doctor.

Miss a meal—or two—or three.
Sleep in a tent, a mission, a doorway.

A life as easily erased as the slip of a pencil.
Eyes that once looked at me now look past me.
Seven billion people in the world,
And not one to call my friend.

De nada

With acknowledgements to
St. Matthew's gospel.

Breads by 3268zauber

You fed me when I was hungry,
Clothed me when I was naked.
When I was thirsty you gave me a drink.
You brought medicine when I was sick.

When I was in prison, you visited me.
You welcomed me into your home.
I said, Thank you.

You said, De nada.

A New Star in the East

Nelson Mandela, photo
© by John Mathew Smith, 2001

Beneath a cross his mother wept
As naked hung the son of man.
His words, "Forgive them," whispered low,
On his disciples' lips lived on,
Envoys, ambassadors of Peace.

"I have a dream" resounded still
from Lincoln's chiseled marble form,
and ordinary people wept
as on a motel balcony
lay Martin, bleeding, hushed, serene.

Embraced by leaping pyre flames
Ignited by a mad man's rage,
Mohandas without anger smiled,
Did not so much as lift a hand,
God in his heart and on his lips.

Mandela, freed from prison's chains,
spurned retribution and revenge,
showed mercy to his prison guards,
and over jagged shards of hate
built Reconciliation Road.

Mandela's thin brown body lay,
Extolled by presidents and kings,
then wove a path in high estate through folk,
linked arm in arm,
in lines as long as China's epic Wall.

Humble people, bathed in tears,
Heard music loud and warm and clear.
Throughout the land rang three clear tones
From tolling bells in steepled skies:
. . . Man-DEL-a . . . Man-DEL-a . . . Man-DEL-a . . .

Six-winged angels marked his path
As Nelson scaled celestial heights,
Still overcoming dark with light.
Mandela's star joined Jesus' star
And Gandhi's star and Martin's star.

Emmanu-El
God With Us

They met Him
in places odd
at unexpected times—
in the morning coolness of a perfect garden,
at an altar built by brothers,
in the building of an ark,
beneath a tree by Abraham's tent,
in Big-Time angel wrestling,
in the voice of an ass,
in a burning bush,
from a witch at Endor,
in a midnight cry to a sleeping child,
while tending sheep,
in a battle with Goliath,
in Mt. Carmel's fiery rain

in the silence of a desert cave,
behind the sarcophagus of good King Uzziah,
in a lion's den,
pinching fruit in an orchard,
in the belly of a great fish,
from a death-defying queen,
in the midst of a flaming furnace,
in a miry prison pit,
in the lowly stable,
beside the Sea of Galilee,
in Gethsemane's midnight darkness,
on a wooden cross,
at the mouth of an empty tomb,
on the dusty road to Emmaus,
in tongues of fire,
on Damascus' desert road,
in lonely exile on Patmos.
For me, it was in FoodMaxx.

FoodMaxx, The Save Mart Companies

In a Benedictine Monastery

St. Catherine's Monastery, Sinai, Egypt by Egghead06

Humpty-Dumpty sat on a wall

Of a refrigerator

Humpty-Dumpty had a great fall

Into the frying pan

All the king's horses and all the king's men

Who rushed into the royal kitchen

Couldn't put Humpty together again

But they enjoyed the eggs Benedictine.

Just Like Me

Maybe God doesn't have arms or legs,
A belly button or a big toe,
But you can bet He's got personality.
He likes good things and doesn't like bad things—
Just like me

God is strong when He needs to be,
Gentle when it's called for.
He loves babies and puppies,
And in a pinch, kittens—
Just like me

Clothes by Gucci, or kitschy,
Miss America, or Mr. Magoo,
Tall or short, skinny or not,
God is not big on appearances—
Just like me.

You can ask God for something,
But if it's an asinine request,
He'll probably say,
"You must be kidding—"
Just like me.

God doesn't sweat the small stuff.
People who annoy Him with petty matters
Should get off their butts
And "just do it—"
Just like me.

God doesn't keep an enemies list;
He knows who His friends are.
He doesn't wait till Christmas to find out
Who's been naughty or nice—
Just like me.

God won't always help you
If you get in a jam.
He might leave you hanging
To teach you a lesson—
Just like me.

If you're dumb enough to tick God off,
He'll take you to the woodshed,
Behind the gym, or under the bleachers,
And teach you a lesson you won't soon forget—
Just like me.

Now that I think of it,
I know a lot about God.
We're not all that different.
God, as it turns out—
Is just like me.

Every God Known to Man

Zeus de Smyrne by
Marie-Lan Nguyen

Not every god has a golden head with fiery eyes,
A raised fist gripping thunderbolts and lightning,
Or a quiver full of never-failing arrows.

Not all have brazen arms and breastplates,
Or girdles of pearl and amethyst.
Not all have legs like giant Sequoias,
Or gossamer robes that sway
To the music of the spheres.

But every god known to man,
Without exception,
Has feet of clay.

King of the Hill

When I
was a boy,
we played a game
called "King of the Hill."
Standing on any small rise,
one boy declared himself "King,"
and the rest of us fought to push him off until
another boy became the "King of the Hill."

Older than god, the King of the Hill
makes the rich richer, and the poor poorer.
He turns a deaf ear when you cry out
in emergency rooms, corporate boardrooms,
at the water cooler, and the ballot box,
in police stations, courtrooms, and rescue missions.

To the King, you are expendable.
You are nine ciphers: 000-00-0000,
a timecard, a necessary liability,
a demographic, a statistic.

He says, “Someone’s got to pick the grapes.”
“Nobody said life was fair.”
“Everybody does it.”
“At least take a shower and shave.”

Once in his ravenous jaws,
you’ll not escape his inward-turned shark’s teeth.
He will drag you down
and pull you under till, at last, you die.

The King has four laws:
The first law: Survive.
The second law: Survive and Pro$per.
The third law: Pro$per some more.
The fourth law: Never share your Hill.

His name is POWER.

The Empty House

Abandoned House, Realty Biz News

No voice speaks; no ear to hear:
"Come to breakfast."
"I love you a bushel and a peck."
"Dessert is for kids who eat their peas."
"Is your homework done?"
"Sleep tight. Don't let the bedbugs bite."

Walls that witnessed life and love stand mute,
Well-used doors hang motionless,
Shades are drawn, the light is dim.
Silence fills the house
With everything—and with nothing.

A Portrait Artist

Through the years he had painted
people as he saw them.
Patrons murmured,
"Somber tones," "Shadows, deep."
He wondered,
but painted still.

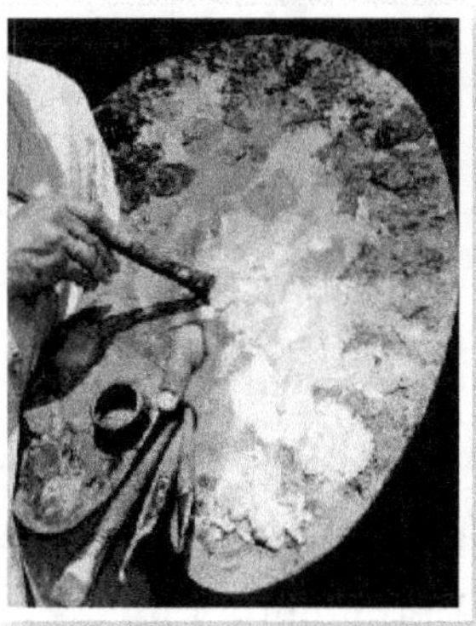

Musing in his studio,
he cried out with a gasp.
Reflected in a silvered glass,
Himself he had painted,
his pain,
his sorrows dark.

Teardrops

Depressed man

A single teardrop—
For a peach-tree switch
That stung my legs,
And for the dear heart
Who wielded it.

A rivulet of regret—
For time in academia,
Completing the courses
But not knowing
I did not know.

A brook—
Tumbling over boulders
For lives I failed to touch,
For hearts whose pulse I never felt.

A once-in-a-lifetime deluge—
For the love I should have given,
And received,
But didn't.

An ocean of briny tears—
Stretching beyond the horizon
Into the Unknown.

My 23rd Song

A Paraphrase

The Good Shepherd

The Lord is my shepherd;
He takes good care of me.
He helps me find food and shelter,
He gives me peace within,
He makes me feel alive again,
He helps me to do the right thing.

When I face life's darkest moments,
I can still have courage
Because you are with me.
Your presence puts my mind at ease.

Picture a royal reception.
While everyone watches,
You summon me to the head table.
I drink from a bottomless cup!

His goodness and mercy are my constant companions,
And I will be a part of God's family forever.

On a Warm Summer Day

Sorting darks from whites,
Jane added brighteners,
Making sure the load was full,
Drying on GENTLE on a hot summer day,
As I, holding back the tears, lay dying.

Waiting in line at vacuum pumps,
Michael used a dollar-off coupon,
Watched attendants wipe the tires.
Planning to leave a large tip—
As I, with no use for money, lay dying.

Susan chose fresh orange juice,
Passed up frozen entrees,
Took a cake mix on impulse,
Prayed the checkout lines were short,
As I, with taste buds gone, lay dying.

Shining faces pledged allegiance
To the flag of the United States of America
And to the Republic for which it stands,
One nation, under God—
As I, with pain well masked, lay dying.

Robert made the great room greater,
Designed grand entryways,
Enlarged pantries for more storage,
While I lamented the pain I brought my family,
As I lay dying.

My life is slowly slipping away
Like sand through a child's fingers.
I console my heart with memories,
Humming, "Jesus doeth all things well,"
As I lie weeping, dying.

In a war no one has ever won,
My only armor, a patchwork quilt,
My will concedes the battle.
Still my heart says yes to hope and life—
As I lie dying on a warm summer day.

What to Wear?

Death Riding a Pony

Death
Rises,
Yawns,
Opens his closet.
What to wear today?
Traditional black? Or colors more chic?

In white-hooded robe,
A scythe on his shoulders,
Death knocks politely, ever so politely.
No rush.
No hurry.

On a windy day,
In pale pinks and blues,
Death,
Like a playmate,
Puts away the toys and departs, but not alone.

A father pleads,
"Take me instead,"
But Death ignores his plea,
tightens his grip on an only son,
Leaving behind a man bathed in tears.

Death has seen this before:
A father and his daughter
Saying goodbye,
Heartbeat visible
Beneath a cotton sheet.

Drums roll, trumpets blare, the battle is joined.
From atop a red mount,
Death
Harvests heroes
From both armies.

"I'm your flight steward.
Window seat or aisle?
Buckle your seatbelts.
Your captain today
Is Mortality."

Searching for G.W.D.

A man and two women
Emerged from a rented car,
Wandered through Caney Cemetery
Under a boiling Kansas sun
In search of some sign of George Washington Davis,
Coming to an upright stone
Caked with green and orange moss,
Longing to recover faded names and dates,
Covering faint lines with paper,
Rubbing its face with lead pencil,
Harvested its only remaining words:

GONE, BUT NOT FORGOTTEN.

Ode to Silence

1998-2002 Lincoln Town Car limousine

Hush!

Elizabeth Taylor has died.
Escorted by white, stretch limos that seat twenty,
In an intimate, private ceremony,
She was interred at Forest Lawn Cemetery
Alongside other stars
Whose lights outshone the night sky.
Her name the first word spoken on every newscast.

Other great and good have died
Whose names were not even whispered—

By anyone.

Seize the Moment

With light fully banished,
Thunderheads clash in heaven's arena.
The firmament splits and atoms explode
Like a master magician lighting up the Earth.
The towering majesty and fearful force
Etch images on the eye and on the memory.

Predestined to fail, cameras click away.
Looking at the snapshot, the viewer mutters,
"Nice."
The excitement is past,
It will no more return
Than a river will flow backward.

Country

Acoustic guitar

Gimme a song that tells a story
and touches my heart,
a song about Momma
makin' herself a dress outta flower sacks,
and one for Rose to wear to school.
She never got a day off, not even Sundays.
Had supper on the table when Daddy come home.
A few times I saw him hug her in front of us.
Whenever he took Momma dancin',
we waited up, long as we could,
hopin' to see 'em happy when they come home.

Daddy wanted to be a singer,
had his guitar and all.
He made-up a good song
about the girl of his dreams,
With blue eyes, from Texas.
Momma said she was that girl.
The man in the song had on cowboy boots,
a western shirt, a pistol at his side,
and a Ranger star on his chest.
Peace lovin' by nature.
Daddy called his song "A Lotta Woman."

A Lotta Woman

<u>Verse:</u> A smile on my lips
but not in my eyes.
Whisperin' sweet nothin's.
Nothin' but lies.

My eyes was wild
Till I met you,
And give my heart
To your eyes of blue.

<u>Chorus:</u> I swore to be true,
As true as I can,
'Cuz you're a lotta woman
For just one man.

<u>Verse:</u> I don't run around
From door to door.
My cheatin' heart
Don't cheat no more.

I never thought
I could be true,
But I'd be cheatin' myself
If I cheated on you.

<u>Chorus</u>: I swore to be true,
As true as I can,
'Cuz you're a lotta woman
For just one man.

There's Jimmy, he weren't right,
but we didn't know nothin' to do.
When he got older, he was strong as a ox.
Girls was afraid around him.
Momma was skeered he might git lost in the woods.
She couldn't stand the thought of Jimmy,
out there all by hisself.

Me? Ain't much to tell.
Walkin' two miles to school 'tweren't no bother.
Eight grades in one room.
Rose was in second.
Me and her walked together.
Sometimes I give her a piggyback ride.
When she fell asleep on her desk,
teacher let her sleep.

Teacher said I figured good.
The world she told us about were like a dream.
Nothin' real about it to me.
I just wanted to git home and have supper.

Lily was three.
She only had a diaper,
'cept in the winter, she had a coat.

We raised Blue from a pup.
He slep' most of the time,
but he loved to hunt.
Shakin' his head, his ears flopped
like leaves on the tree.
Take out the squirrel rifle,
and his eyes 'd light up,
sniffin' and rarin' to go.
When we lost Blue
I didn't cry—
I bawled.
Only time in my life.
Did he run off?
Someone musta stole him.
I miss Blue somethin' awful.

Daddy went down to the mine.
Never saw the sun
'cept a few hours on the Sabbath.
He was a sad, sad man and a mean drunk.
And if he stopped in a honkytonk on his way home
to drown his sorrows in a few beers—
look out.
His soul turned black as the coal he brung up from the earth.

Momma waited up for him,
Knowin' there'd be hell to pay.

The night he left, he come home and washed up.
We ate supper and he sent us to bed.
I heard him sayin' to Momma,
I'm sorry, but I gotta go.
I gotta git outta here before I die.

What about me and the kids?

He said I'm sorry. Here's all I got,
and he emptied his pockets on the bed.
Through a crack, I saw him stuffin' his clothes in a sack.

You're leavin' me and the kids without nothin'?

He begun to cry but kept on packin'.
I'm a dead man if I stay.
I gotta git out.
He put on his jacket,
picked up his guitar, and went out the door.

Watchin' out the window
I saw the old pickup disappear into the night,
leavin' Momma with a hole in her heart.

Momma cried herself to sleep that night.
I heard her prayin' and cryin' at the same time.
I knowed she was on her knees by her bed.

Lord, what'll I do? What'll I do? Lord he'p me.
You know the fix we're in.

The springs squeaked when she finally got in bed.
I thought she would never stop cryin'.
The preacher said he prayed for us,
but he was as poor as us people in the holler.
He had his own to take care of.

He said Jesus might help us,
but I never saw him in our neck of the woods.

Momma scraped till her fingers was raw.
But it weren't enough.
She opened the cabinet doors one by one.
She sold everythin' she could,
till we didn't have nothin' nobody wanted.
We didn't know where to turn.

Three months since my Daddy left,
Floyd the sheriff's assistant, a deputy or somethin',
came sniffin' around.
When he grinned, looked like a possum
with a mouth full of teeth.
The preacher told us about Satan temptin' Jesus.
Floyd was Satan come to tempt Momma.

We was all hungry.
Floyd, too.
He set two sacks on the table
and set down like he belonged.

Momma looked at Floyd steady.
She looked at Jimmy, and me, and Rose and Lily.
She stared at the groceries.
Finally, she whispered,

I'll git supper.
She did not smile.

* * *

Driving through the woods in my 4x4,
I spot the gray unpainted siding and stop to stare.
For no reason I know of,
I'm walking toward the old house.
It's hard to breathe, like I'm carrying a heavy weight,
my heart beating like a bass drum.

Momma's gone. Jimmie's gone.
Rose and Lily have families
I can't quit thinking
How Momma cried the night Daddy left.

I remember her eyes of blue
And what Momma did for us.
I don't cry anymore.
I'm all cried out.

Who You Sleepin' with Tonight?

Hey, Buddy! How's it going?
 Pretty good for a Monday.
Do any business today?
 Yeah. Pretty good day at the mall.
 Their security people get dumber every year.
Through for the day?
 Yep. Supper, TV, and bed—alone.
What happened to Dolly?
 I got tired of her and passed her over to Jamal.
What about Pearl? She still around?
 She turned out to be a nagger. I sent her packing.

Well, at least you've got a mutt to keep you company.

Rocky's got fleas.

He's sleeping under the porch tonight.

So, who's left?

I guess I'll sleep with myself.

Sleeping with your Self. That must be godawful.

I won't get much sleep.

Can't send your Self away, can you?

Tell me about it.

Dog

Pity the Pig

Yorkshire pigs wallow in mud at the Poplar Spring Animal Sanctuary in Poolesville, Maryland, by Mark Peters

Can a pig his sty make neat?
Will he tidy up the floor?
Must he wallow in the muck
unheeding of the oozing stench?
Must he push aside his mates,
gorge himself, and eat his fill?

If you neaten up his sty,
he will mess it up again.
If you tidy up the floor,
he will strew it with his waste
till its aroma again smells sweet
to his inquiring snout.

Never to search for unknown worlds,
to sing a song, or write a book,
or chuckle at a well-timed joke.
Never will he love—or hate,
never be his best—or worst,
never rise above himself.

The Voice of a Daisy

Daisy

She looks at me expressionless.
If only she would smile or wink or nod—
She does none of those.

She sits straight.
If she leans toward me, or shifts in her seat—
She does neither.

She turns away, then back.
If she raises an eyebrow, or parts her lips—
She gives no signal.

She straightens her shoulders.
If she extends a hand, or turns her gaze—
She is like a statue.

She pushes her hair back over one ear.
If her falling hand reaches out to me—
It does not.

She sits hands folded in her lap,
Like a lighthouse on a calm night.
Does her heart beat for me?

I must know or die.
"She loves me; she loves me not.
She loves me; she loves me not."

"She loves me!"
I can't believe it! She loves me!
SHE LOVES ME!

Proverbs 31

In honor of my wife and my mother

Can you spot a good woman,
One you wouldn't trade for "all the tea in China?"
Her mate trusts her
And is never disappointed.
She's a valued partner for as long as she lives.

She starts her day early,
Seeing that her family is fed and clothed.
She manages her household
And spends money wisely.

She is not afraid of hard work.
She knows the value of her contribution
And doesn't quit till the job is done.
She takes cares of her own family
But doesn't ignore the needy.

Everything she does, she does well.
She has the poise of a queen.
She doesn't fret about the future.
She makes sense when she talks,
Speaks in a kindly manner,
And makes good use of her time.

Her children say, "We're lucky she's our mom."
Her spouse brags about her.
"Other women have their good points,
But you're number one!"

Smiles can fool you, and beauty is only skin deep,
But a woman who honors God is a keeper.
Everybody respects her,
Her good reputation is well deserved.

On the Front Porch

VEIKOUS Outdoor Wooden Porch Swing, Overstock

On the hottest day
In Oklahoma history,
With no shade or air conditioning,
In the grip of a cruel sun,

Shoes cast off—it wasn't Sunday—
Shirt, unnecessary baggage,
In cutoffs we called short pants,
I lay on my back

In a gray painted wooden swing
Made by my father's own hands,
Suspended in air by link chains
From rafters on our tiny porch.

Heat, like a merciless mother,
Pulled earth to her bosom,
Clasping creatures in a death grip,
Daring living things to breathe,

When, like a gentle lover,
A puff of wind
Stole across my flesh—
and was gone.

On a Chinese Elm

Chinese Elm by Ronnie Nijboer

Spring juices bid buds come out to play
With comrades along the branches.
Leaves play tug-of-war with March's gusting winds,
Bathe in sweet April showers,
Block the onslaught of summer sun,
And hide a child from his mother's eyes.

Then in the face of chilling autumn winds,
Green converts to scarlet and miser's gold.
And one by one, playmates drift to earth
Till the last one loses its grip,
Leaving space for Spring and hope.

Puns with ESL Names

It's a joy teaching ESL students,
Whose names reflect various cultures,
But what Americans do to foreigners' names
Is normally done by vultures.

Yet even teachers who practice the names
Hear things that sound sort of funny,
If the names below sound like fun and games,
It's mostly because they are punny.

We have a boy named MA, a girl named PA,
Three boys in one class named SUE.
HER is a him, HEM is a her,
A ME, a MAI, and a YEU.

A MAN who's a lady, a childless MOM,
A TORNH who can SING a SONG,

A CESAR not a salad, A ROMAN not Italian,
Two cooks (KOK, CUOC), and a LAO who is Hmong.

Turn steak with a NOUTHONG, savor the TAING,
Shake hands with a Lao named SAIGON.
If you wish for a fish, we feature LITHOUNA,
Served gladly by a tiny KINGKHAM.

Hey, diddle, diddle, try a math riddle.
What will your answer be?
Add LE, to a LEE, and TOU LEE, too.
The answer's not four LEE'S, but three.

For religious folk of King James persuasion,
There's a YEE, a NAY, and a LO!
From Genesis' LABEN to the gospel of MARK,
From ALPHA to his sister, OMEGA.

A first-class princess, whose family is POR,
But the student from Georgia's just PHO,
A BEE with no sting, a LOC, but no door,
A kid five feet tall who is LO.

A KER, a HER, a DER, and a GER,
A PO, KHO, LO, and a ME,
A VANG, a PANG, a HANG, SANG, YANG,
A GEE—and a BEE, VEE, DY.

A CHAK who can talk, a CHUM who's a pal,
Two boys, when they're old still NOU,
If you're lost, CHEK our MAP, but don't look around
For Buster Brown's THY in your shoe.

A poem, like a sundae, is finally complete
When a red cherry crowns the top.
Two student names, NAN-THA-VONG-DOUANG-SY,
And IN-PRA-VONG-VIENG-KHAM, share that spot.

There's MOR, much more, but I don't want to bore,
Or try any tricks to amaze you.
I'll end with a boy who is really a KAO,
And an OLAY! from Southeast Asia.

The Weight of a Word

Scale PNG Clipart, PNG ALL

Eager and *anxious* are heavy,
One with seeds of joy,
the other, clouds of doubt.
Hate is heavy, like its brutish brothers,
Loathe, detest, despise, abhor.
Some words awaken tears:
Bereavement, trauma, alienation.

Intent on harm, *Letter* words weigh a ton:
The N-word, the Q-word, the F-word—pick a letter.
Like stones, words are hurled at protesters,
Fallen women, traitorous men, and saints.
Words flood the air with hurricanes of nonsense,
And weigh enough to crush the soul.

Some words bubble with delight:
Effervescence, sparkle, fizz, zest.
Some words caress the senses:
A *still* pond, a *serene* smile, a *tranquil* spirit.
Some are crafty:
Sly as a fox, *forked-tongue*, *two-faced.*

L*ove* is a fickle favorite:
Love ya, *love* pets, *love* chocolate cake,
Love rainbows, and the color purple.
Silver and platinum are precious,
As are *jewels in a pirate's treasure trove.*
Words can lift the spirit, liberate the mind,
And free those yet unborn to seek the light.

Love, Truth, and Justice

We make much of Love—
A hospital visit, a shared ride,
A neighborhood barbeque.

    But if you're down on your luck,
    Tough Love takes control
    And decides what's best for you.

Truth between friends
Binds heart to heart
And gives a warm embrace.

    But drawn from creed and dogma,
    Truth says, "Chapter and verse,
    Or you're out of the club."

Justice stands up to a bully,
Makes sure the little one gets a turn,
Knows there are always two sides.

But in court, Justice stares you down
And pronounces judgment:
"You should have read the fine print."

Love, Truth, and Justice—
From within: unrivaled gems,
Pink diamonds.

From without: they take control,
Build walls, haul you into court,
And rob you of your humanity.

Walls

Fence along Commerce Blvd at the Raleigh-Durham International Airport by Ildar Sagdejev (Specious)

A wall says,
"You're not welcome."
"You have no seat on the board."
"This land is posted: Keep Out."

Walls never say,
"There's plenty for all."
"Color doesn't matter."
"Here's your ballot."

Walls writ into law fall to voting machines,
And if not voting machines,
To revolution,
violent and non-violent.

When a wall blocks your path,
If you have the will to fight
And no fear of dying,
You can take it down—
Alone, or with others,
One stone at a time,
Hack, hack, hack.

The Great Wall of China was breached.
The Berlin Wall fell to the wrecker's ball.
Cutters snipped through barbed wire walls.
Walls of white gave way to Selma marchers.

The world is a maze
With a thousand thousand walls,
Bearing names like Narcissism, Egotism,
Sexism, Pride, Hypocrisy, Ignorance,
Nation-Building, Organized Religion, and more.

No matter how artfully applied the makeup,
How chic the outward attire,
How cultured or well-mannered,
Walls throb with an insatiable lust
For dominance, for lordship,
For the power of life or death
Over any and all challengers.

I Corinthians

If I preached like Peter at Pentecost, but without love,
It means about the same as the noise of tin cans
Dragging behind the newlywed's car.

If I tell people about God,
and understand the Second Coming,
And have faith so I could spin a mountain like a top,
but lack love,
I'm still standing on square one.

If I give away everything, even my life,
But do it without love,
It's all a big, fat zero.

Love gives others the benefit of the doubt
and is respectful.
Love isn't possessive and doesn't gloat
(even about grandchildren).
Love doesn't look down its nose at anyone.

It isn't always demanding its rights;
It's not cranky or unfriendly.
It's saddened by people's bad luck
but elated by their good fortune.

Love suffers without whining,
Believes in others, hopes for the best,
Endures like a good soldier.

Love lasts.

Though some sermons seem endless,
they will cease;
Charismatic outpourings will end;
Our best knowledge will end up in a shredder,

Because knowledge is like a page in the wind,
And our preaching, well—
No one has to be told that's imperfect.

But when perfection arrives,
All our half-baked efforts will crumble
Like the walls of Jericho.

When I was little, I babbled like a child.
I reasoned like a child
And thought only of myself.
But I've outgrown that.

Now, it's like watching an eclipse
Through a piece of smoked glass.
Then, all will be crystal clear.

Now, we have little slivers of light—
Then, we'll see fully and clearly
Just as we are seen fully and clearly now.

So, there's faith, hope, and love,
All thoroughbreds,
But faith and hope
Will still be coming down the homestretch
When love has already crossed the finish line.

Images

Page

1. Placing a Wedding Ring, photo by Petar Milošević / http://bit.ly/3TLmdm8/ CC BY-SA 4.0
3. Tadpole, Nature Study: Raising Tadpoles with Kids / http://bit.ly/3JlGw4F
4. Tree frog, LEGO education, Frog's Metamorphosis, Lesson 8 of 20 / http://bit.ly/3Jo2qEu
6. OZ Goose Sailing Dinghy / https://www.opengoose.com/
10. Fall Foliage Colors Lake Reflections, West Virginia, by ForestWander / CC BY-SA 3.0 US / http://bit.ly/3FzJr8y
18. Skein of pink-footed geese in 'V'.jpg, by Apricaria / CC BY-SA 4.0 / https://bit.ly/43Hv1gi
20. Passer domesticus flying, by SimonWaldherr / SA 4.0 International / http://bit.ly/3GrhTTn
24. Ford Bronco Raptor / http://bit.ly/3JVLB5n
27. Retired Col. Dick Camp, author of "The Devil Dogs at Belleau Wood," speaks with Sgts. Ricardo Quintanilla, Brandon McCormick and Jarred Bluecoat about Marines who fought in the World War I battle at Belleau Wood, photo by Sgt. Lisa R. Strickland / Public Domain / http://bit.ly/3Ekv1c7
30. A Czech soldier with the 1st Company, 41st Mechanized Infantry Battalion carries a U.S. Soldier with the 173rd Airborne Brigade Combat Team Sept. 2, 2014, during Saber Junction 2014 at the Joint Multinational Readiness Center in Hohenfels, Germany. Saber

Junction is a U.S. Army Europe-led exercise designed to prepare U.S., NATO and international partner forces for unified land operations, photo by SPC Tyler Kingsbury / defenseimagery.mil / Public Domain / http://bit.ly/3lQIYYC

32. A red devil cartoon character with facial expression Free Vector / <a href=“https://www.vecteezy.com/free-vector/red”>c by Vecteezy</a> / https://bit.ly/3EnO854

33. Times Square New Year's celebration, Dec. 31, 2011, at The One Times Square Building, New York, NY, US, by Nichole A. Hall / Public Domain / http://bit.ly/3KnigBg

35. Photo by Bob Smith / https://normalbob.com

37. Breads, by 3268zauber / GNU FDL / http://bit.ly/3Ss8obD

39. From Wash D.C. Longworth building October 4, 1994. Mandela's first trip to the United States, © copyright John Mathew Smith 2001 / CC BY-SA 2.0 / http://bit.ly/3YZ899o

43. FoodMaxx, The Save Mart Companies / Winsight Grocery Business / http://bit.ly/3liG9jp

44. Panoramic view of St. Catherine's Monastery, Sinai, Egypt, by Egghead06 / Public Domain / http://bit.ly/3xyXzdQ

49. Zeus de Smyrne, by Marie-Lan Nguyen / Public Domain / http://bit.ly/3FvUn7d

53. Abandoned house, Realty Biz News, Real Estate Investing, FINDING ABANDONED HOUSES FOR INVESTING / http://bit.ly/3mYqJRQ

55. Oil painting palette, by Max Wehlte / English Wikipedia / Public Domain / http://bit.ly/3TqNqdE

56. What are the Signs, Symptoms, Causes and Treatment for Depression in Men? / MidValley Healthcare / http://bit.ly/3lPhJOk

58. The Good Shepherd / https://journey2joyblog.com/2017/03/

62. Death riding a pony vector clip art / Public Domain / http://bit.ly/3mTBzIJ

66. 1998-2002 Lincoln Town Car limousine, by IFCAR / Public Domain / http://bit.ly/3ZXgpYQ

68. Acoustic guitar, PLAY GUITARS, The Top 10 Ways to Practice Acoustic Guitar Techniques / http://bit.ly/3leKSCJ

79. Dog, Mange In Dogs: Symptoms, Treatment & Prevention, Tractive / http://bit.ly/3JL8N5V

80. Yorkshire pigs wallow in mud at the Poplar Spring Animal Sanctuary in Poolesville, Maryland, by Mark Peters, Baltimore, USA (cropped) / CC BY-SA 2.0 / http://bit.ly/3YUJkeE

82. Daisy, April Birth Flower, AvasFlowers / http://bit.ly/3lgQ1u2

86. VEIKOUS Outdoor Wooden Porch Swing, Overstock / http://bit.ly/3lDa45t

88. Chinese elm, by Ronnie Nijboer / CC0 1.0 Universal Public Domain / http://bit.ly/3ICbMx5

93. Scale PNG Clipart, PNG ALL / CC BY-NC 4.0 /http://bit.ly/3yLDq5a

97. Fence along Commerce Blvd at the Raleigh-Durham International Airport, by Ildar Sagdejev (Specious), CC BY-SA 4.0 / http://bit.ly/3xz7Kiz

108. FROG LEGS: Short Stories About Life, by Wayland Bryant Jackson / https://amzn.to/3YKWxrd

110. WHEN GOD DISAPPEARED . . . and Where God Showed Up, by Wayland Bryant Jackson / https://amzn.to/3ZlqdKV

121. Photo of Wayland Bryant Jackson

Acknowledgment

My deepest gratitude to the editor, Holly Thompson,
And to our previewers who were off to the races with
their insights, kindness, and enthusiasm:

Julia Rux
Deborah Homan Still
Michael Haensel . . . Bill Simmons
Seth Stuart . . . Devine Davis-Williams
Rob Hertzenberg . . . Rebecca Dolence
Rhonda Herb . . . John Jackson
Marianna Sidiropoulou
John Thompson

More from the Author

Available Now!

What's inside FROG LEGS . . .

children playing "Funeral"
a child afraid of the dark
a boy loses his mother and meets God
a student handles harassment
a teen's first date and the connection between sex & love
a young adult longing to leave the nest

"the bended knee" and racial inequality
a woman counters a dealer's bait-and-switch tactics
a young aide in a nursing home who finds a gift
a hitchhiker challenges the practice of shunning
a professor meets a genie

the perils of pride
a professor rides the slippery slope to murder
wonder at a church's inclusion of a homeless woman
a fix-it disaster

a Spirit describes the walls that divide us
a crazy cowboy's jump of his life
a wife finds her power
a country girl haunted by her family's hard times

a senior trades bodies with a younger man
a father intervenes for his adult children
a sojourner reflects on the Good Book
a tavern puts God on trial, and
an old man waiting for death reflects on his life.

Also from the Author

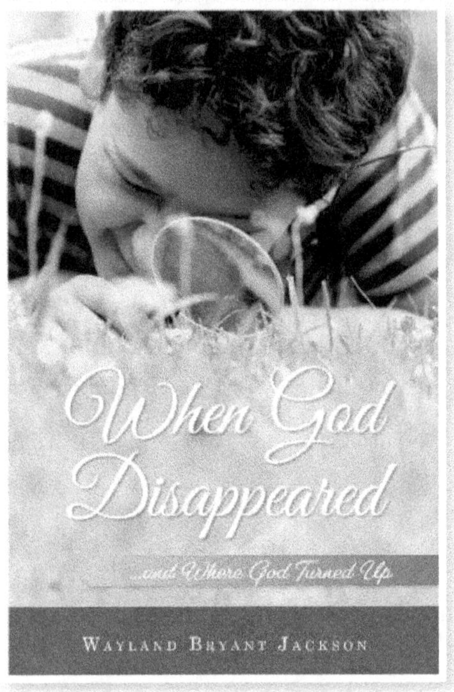

Confused? To disappear can mean different things: One, you just go in the other room and disappear. Two, you vanish in a magician's trick—poof! Three is something else entirely. Read my memoir to see what it meant for me When God Disappeared.

–Wayland Bryant Jackson

Available Now!

WHEN GOD DISAPPEARED
. . . and Where God Turned Up

Excerpt from Chapter 7
Fitted for a Suit of Armor

. . . Each worship service ended with an invitation—the singing of a hymn during which people were encouraged to declare their faith. I wanted to belong, but the thought of standing before the church was daunting. Everyone there was a member. I wasn't. I felt the pastor's piercing eye, so I began leaving by the back door to avoid making eye contact with him at the close of the services.

Boen Halum, a red-headed, guitar-strumming evangelist, held a series of nightly meetings—a revival—at K Street. On Saturday evening . . . with a single step out of the pew into the aisle, my guilt vanished, guilt for being different, for not being a part of the group, for being a sinner. When I shook his hand, the pastor didn't ask if I believed in God or Jesus, or if I repented of my sins. Good thing, because the joy I felt came from being rid of my guilt. He asked me if I were transferring my membership. I said yes, and he seemed satisfied . . .

Joining the church meant more than getting my name on the roll. It meant people, adults outside my biological family, accepted me. I found a new family and new friends. I learned to talk like they talked and think like they thought, not unlike a teenager joining a gang. Our "gang" was saved, and we knew it. Our mission was to study the Bible and spread the word. The world needed us and our God.

I accepted a basic Christian assumption: we are sinners. Not just flawed or imperfect, not clumsy, or ignorant or misguided, but sinners. Life was defined by a religious term. To Baptists, conversion isn't a caterpillar becoming a butterfly. It's a worm crawling out of the ground into the sunlight, grateful that grace "saved a wretch like me," but still a worm . . .

From Chapter 8
Boot Camp

. . . Dan Tyson, the area missionary for southern Oklahoma, loaded our luggage into his car and gave me and Dorothy Kyker, a student from a small town near Ardmore, the 100-mile ride to Shawnee, home of the Oklahoma Baptist University Bison. After dropping Dorothy off at the women's Memorial Dormitory, he left me about a half-mile south at an abandoned two-story Navy barracks used for male student overflow.

The first night I was scared and considered running away. But when I awoke in the morning, I felt better. I soon got busy trying to figure out the job of being a student: enrolling, choosing classes, living off-campus, making my bed, passing room checks, showering in a community bath, standing in chow lines, acquiring books, and doing P. E. . . .

A new star had risen in the East. I hitched a ride with a few guys traveling to Oklahoma City to attend the Billy Graham Evangelistic Crusade. Baptists were excited because he was one of us. Before Graham spoke, George Beverly Shea led a choir of hundreds singing "How Great Thou Art?" captivating an audience of thousands.

Graham's simple message, delivered with his endearing accent and Southern charm, swept the nation. He preached a simple, accessible gospel, a contract offered by God: Believe in Jesus, walk the "sawdust trail," step forward, talk to a counselor, "Sign here," and you could go home a born-again Christian. Fundamentalism became socially acceptable, and all the major media from shore to shore loved us. We were not only right, we were fashionable, and I was part of the in-crowd . . .

At OBU, racism was a silent normal. The university accepted blacks—if they were from Nigeria—Hispanics from Cuba, and Orientals only from China. After graduating, Jorge would return to his well-to-do family in Cuba. However, Stuart Wu, a pre-med student from China, faced a more difficult choice. After Mao Tse Tung's revolution, China was now officially atheist, and Stuart was a Baptist.

"What will you do?" I asked him.

"I'll return to help my people," he said. No matter how he felt inside, his face showed no emotion. In the meantime, he had no way of knowing what was happening to his family in China. Risk and danger marked every scenario he could imagine.

From Chapter 9
Maneuvers

. . . That summer, my Granny Jack (Jackson) lay dying in my aunt and uncle's home in Ardmore. I paid her the respectful visit. She raised her head from the pillow and asked, "Are you Semore?"

"No, Granny. I'm Wayland, Semore's son."

Her head went back down on the pillow for a few seconds. She raised it again and asked, "You're a Baptist, aren't you?"

"Yes, Granny," I confessed.

Her head went back down for a few seconds, then she looked me in the eye and said matter-of-factly, "You know you're going to hell when you die."

Close to her own death, she was concerned for the soul of her grandson. According to Baptist theology, I could have passed the same judgment on Granny, but I would never do that.

Available wherever books are sold!

Coming Soon!

17

Things Your Pastor Will Never Tell You

So, did you know?

- The Bible contains more than one creation story.
- The first recorded perpetrator of genocide is not who you'd think.
- A satan is a whole nother thing.
- You wouldn't be the first to think Judas should've had a choice in the matter.
- Open marriage was fine by Corinthian Christians.
- Tithing is not a Christian practice.
- Plagiarism was okay when sacred texts were being written.
- There is no formula in the Bible for salvation.
- Gehenna was a hot spot.
- Christians had no Bible for over 350 years; the Bible is not *a* book; it doesn't claim to be Inspired; and it has contradictions. Let's unpack that!

- There are things the Bible says to do that we will never ever do, no matter what the Bible orders—nor should we.
- Science and Faith are neither friends nor enemies but as for the existence of God, there is no scientific proof.
- Instead of setting themselves apart and judging us, preachers can include themselves in the collective with one little word.

And more!

Wonderful things can happen when we approach life with an open mind. So, as you read my "revelations," feel free to disagree at any point. My only request is that if you disagree, you do it for any reason other than "That's what I've always believed" or "This is not what my church teaches." Instead, be open to the possibility that so long as we breathe, each of us can learn and grow.

You may ask where a writer like me, who is neither a prophet nor the son of a prophet, neither a scholar nor the son of a scholar, and with no degree in anthropology or archaeology, gets the effrontery to write about ancient dead languages and cultures that are millennia in the past as if I know anything.

To set the reader's mind at ease, I will disclose that I have a bachelor's and a master's degree from an accredited university and a seminary, as well as a teaching credential, but I'm well aware that a degree may not be worth the paper it's written on. In my lifetime, I have been exposed to (not studied) five languages other than English. They are Latin, Greek, Hebrew, Spanish, and German. However, not being a scholar, I made no notes and have almost no recollection of where many of my ideas originated. I read, draw conclusions, and write, and I will happily learn from anyone with documentation that contradicts a single word or sentence herein.

I begin by affirming my affection for that icon of Western culture, the Bible. Passages in the King James Version reach heights rarely equaled in the English language—the 23rd Psalm, the creation story in Genesis 1, the love poem in 1 Corinthians 13; the celebration of the love of God in Romans 8, the Sermon on the Mount with the Beatitudes, and others. However, to be honest, there are some parts of the Bible, the book of Numbers, for example, I find almost useless. Perhaps a Jewish person might have feelings for these chapters, but I skip quickly over litanies of *who* begat *who* begat *who* begat *who*, as only my genealogy is interesting to me.

By and large, I see ministers, priests, rabbis, gurus, and imams as sincere people who exercise a divine calling to lead others to accept and grow in their faith. Most have genuine faith and do their work with compassion. There are exceptions that make headlines—for that reason. They are exceptions, not the rule.

So, when I suggest an idea the reader might never hear from a minister or priest, the natural question is: *Why not?* Most ministers have degrees of one kind or another and have had some formal education and training for their work. Even so, formal training or not, none of us is free from our culture. We are often locked into assumptions that may become as much a part of our faith as a creed furnished by a religious organization. As an example, many churches display an American flag in their sanctuary. Yet, the American flag has nothing to do with Christianity. Each age has assumptions that are taken as "gospel truth" that should be questioned, even at great cost to the questioner.

Religions based on "revealed" truth major on monologues (the sermon, the ritual)—one-way talks. They focus on answers, not questions. However, Jon Meacham once wrote, "The unexamined faith is not worth believing." I have reaped a bounteous harvest from examining my beliefs and, because I rely heavily on dialogue, I hope you will join me in this journey.

Visit My Website

Short Stories, Essays, Videos, Poetry & Art

https://waylandjackson.com/

If you feel like responding
to any of my writings, please email me:

jacksonwayland48@gmail.com

I will write back.

About Wayland Bryant Jackson

Wayland Bryant Jackson

Author Wayland Bryant Jackson, born in 1931 in southern Oklahoma, migrated to California in 1952. Married 62 years to Betty Jane Hollandsworth Owens Jackson (1930 – 2016), they bore five loving children, who bore six grandchildren, and seven great-grandchildren. A graduate of Oklahoma Baptist University and Golden Gate Baptist Theological Seminary, Wayland is a retired public-school teacher living in Fresno, CA.

Having spent his early years as a Southern Baptist music minister, Jackson shed the trappings of organized religion, but maintained a passion for religious philosophy. Although he didn't start writing until he was in his 80's, now, in his 90's, he's published a family history, a memoir, a book of short stories, and this book of poetry. A regular contributor of social commentary, his Letters to the Editor of the Fresno Bee are legendary for the creative ways he gets straight to the heart of a matter and incentivizes readers to take a loving path forward. Perhaps he was right, after all, to switch his major in college from Piano to English.

On a journey that places a higher value on questions than answers, Jackson revels in theological discussions and welcomes doubt. He balances his observations on "The Ugly Side of God," with "Emmanu-El God with Us," a recitation of the many odd places and unexpected times God's presence has been felt, including his own amazing experience at FoodMaxx.

www.ingramcontent.com/pod-product-compliance
Lightning Source LLC
LaVergne TN
LVHW010109170826
845678LV00012B/2314

* 9 7 9 8 8 2 2 9 1 4 9 1 9 *